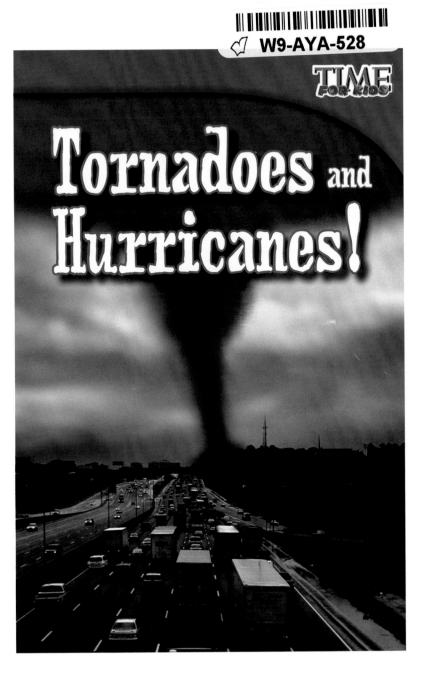

Tornadoes and Hurricanes!

Cy Armour

Consultant

Timothy Rasinski, Ph.D.
Kent State University

Publishing Credits

Dona Herweck Rice, *Editor-in-Chief*
Robin Erickson, *Production Director*
Lee Aucoin, *Creative Director*
Conni Medina, M.A.Ed., *Editorial Director*
Jamey Acosta, *Editor*
Stephanie Reid, *Photo Editor*
Rachelle Cracchiolo, M.S.Ed., *Publisher*

Image Credits

Cover & p.1 Plus Pix/Photolibrary.com; p.3 Anastasios Kandris/Shutterstock; p.4 Enrico Fianchini/ iStockphoto; p.5 top: Mike Theiss/Jim Reed Photography/Photo Researchers, Inc.; p.5 bottom: Westend61/ Photolibrary; p.6 James Thew/Shutterstock; p.7 MCT/Newscom; p.8 top: Christian Delbert/Dreamstime; p.8 bottom: Denis Larkin/Shutterstock; p.9 top: SeanMartin/iStockphoto; p.9 bottom: Illustration by Joe Lertola/www.joelertola.com; p.10 Pete Draper/iStockphoto; p.11 Martin Haas/Shutterstock; p.12 Gary Hincks/Science Photo Library; p.13 Fotolotti/Dreamstime; p.14 Ross Tuckerman/AFP/Getty Images/Newscom; p.15 top: Zoran Ivanovich Photo/iStockphoto; p.15 bottom: EmiliaU/Shutterstock; p.16 Cartesia; p.17 Matt Trommer/Shutterstock; p.18 GWImages/Shutterstock; p.19 Barbara Reddoch/ Dreamstime; p.20-21 Illustration by Joe Lertola/www.joelertola.com; p. 22 Zastol`skiy Victor Leonidovich/ Shutterstock; p.23 Sandra Cunningham/Shutterstock; back cover nautilus_shell_studio/iStockphoto

Based on writing from *TIME For Kids*.

TIME For Kids and the *TIME For Kids* logo are registered trademarks of TIME Inc. Used under license.

Teacher Created Materials

5301 Oceanus Drive
Huntington Beach, CA 92649-1030
http://www.tcmpub.com
ISBN 978-1-4333-3614-0
© 2012 by Teacher Created Materials, Inc.

Table of Contents

Wind Power

    Can you remember blowing on a pinwheel? The harder you blew, the faster it spun.

Imagine thousands of people blowing on that same pinwheel. What would happen?

All of those people might
create a very big wind.

But even if they blew their hardest, the wind they made would not come close to the power of a **tornado** or **hurricane**. Tornadoes and hurricanes are the biggest winds of all!

Tornadoes

Have you ever watched water go down a drain? It becomes a **whirlpool**.

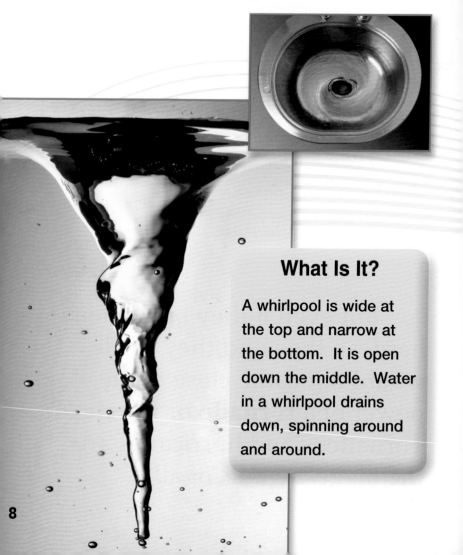

What Is It?

A whirlpool is wide at the top and narrow at the bottom. It is open down the middle. Water in a whirlpool drains down, spinning around and around.

A tornado is like a whirlpool, only it is much bigger and made of air instead of water.

Tornadoes are powerful. If you have seen them in movies, you have some idea of what tornadoes can do.

They can knock down big buildings. They can blow away cars and trees as if they were feathers.

How Tornadoes Happen

Tornadoes come from strong winds, powerful **thunderclouds**, and warm and cold air.

tornado

If warm and cold air meet in a storm, they can form a whirlpool of air. When the whirlpool swirls fast enough, it becomes a tornado.

Debris (duh-BREE) is bits of earth and other things that have been broken and destroyed.

A tornado reaches down from a thundercloud like a swirling, gray snake. It picks up **debris** from the ground below.

The tornado swirls and hops along the ground. It follows the path of the thundercloud.

Tornado winds can reach more than 300 miles per hour!

A tornado can destroy everything in its path. Wind speed makes it very dangerous.

Hurricanes

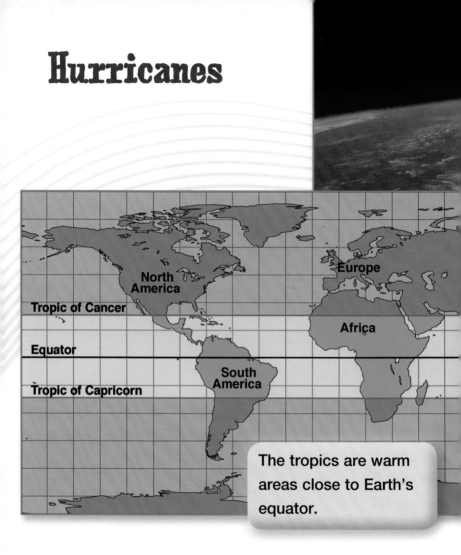

North America

Europe

Tropic of Cancer

Africa

Equator

South America

Tropic of Capricorn

The tropics are warm areas close to Earth's equator.

A hurricane is a powerful storm that begins in ocean **tropics**.

Asia

Australia

Not all hurricanes are called hurricanes. Hurricanes that form over the Pacific Ocean are called typhoons (tahy-FOONS).

The word *hurricane* comes from the name for the Caribbean god of evil, Hurrican. That gives you some idea of a hurricane's terrible power!

How Hurricanes Happen

Most hurricanes start off the west coast of Africa.

If a hurricane is going to form, it needs warm water, moist air, and strong winds that come together from different directions.

When a tropical storm is formed, it is usually given a name, like Tropical Storm Katie. When it becomes a hurricane, it keeps its name.

A hurricane forms in three steps. First, swirling clouds, rain, and wind meet. Next, the wind moves faster to become a **tropical storm**. Last, the wind speeds up to 74 miles per hour or more. Now you have a hurricane!

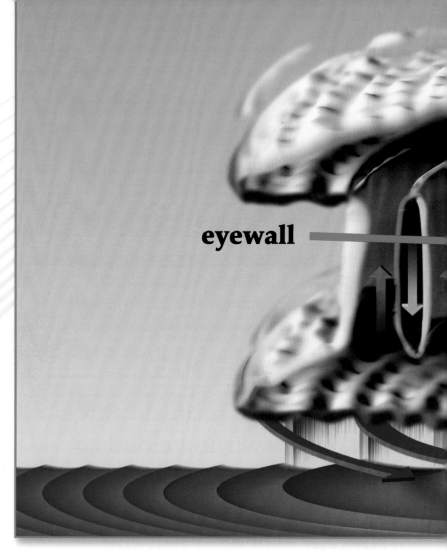

eyewall

Each hurricane has three parts. Its **eye** is the calm center. Fast winds around the eye make the **eyewall**.

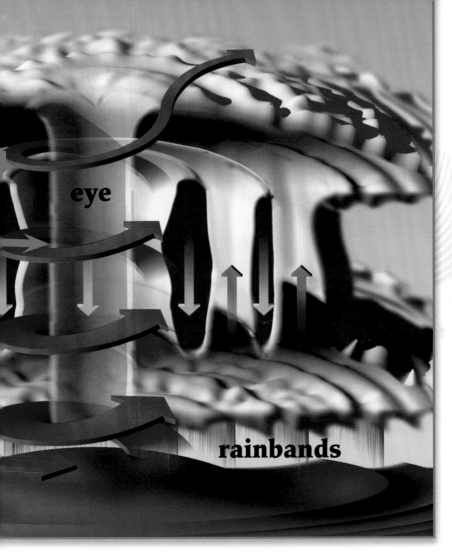

eye

rainbands

Finally, **rainbands** move outward from the eye. They help to keep the storm alive.

Here Comes the Sun

Hurricanes and tornadoes may be powerful. But no matter how strong they are, they must end sometime.

The sun will always come out again!

Glossary

debris—the remains of things that have been broken and destroyed

eye—the calm center of a hurricane

eyewall—a wall of dense thunderclouds

hurricane—a tropical storm that is formed by swirling clouds, rain, and strong winds

rainbands—the parts of the hurricane that keep the storm moving

thunderclouds—large, powerful storm clouds

tornado—a powerful, swirling cloud that reaches to the ground in a cone shape

tropical storm—a storm that happens in the areas of land and water near Earth's equator

tropics—areas of land and water near Earth's equator

whirlpool—a spinning funnel of water with an opening down the center